THE MORMONS

*The Church of Jesus Christ
of Latter-day Saints*

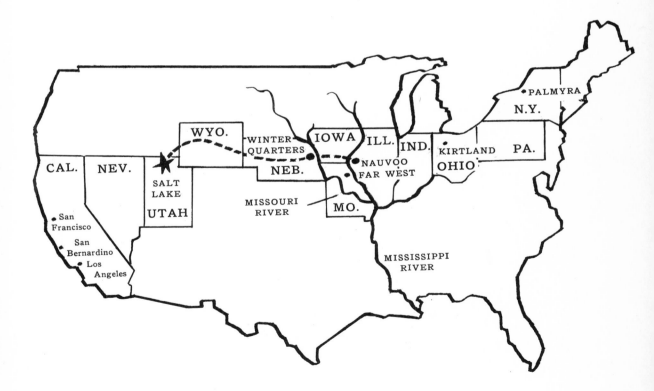

Trail of the Mormon Pioneers — — — — —
1846–47

THE
Freedom to Worship
SERIES

December 15, 1791, First Amendment, Article I, of the Bill of Rights: "Congress shall make no law respecting an establishment of religion, or prohibiting the free exercise thereof."

THE BIRTH of our country created a fresh start for many people; it was the beginning of many new ideas. For one thing, there was no dominance or control by any one religious group. Our government was the *first* in history to pledge complete freedom to worship.

The first ten Amendments to our Constitution were passed on December 15, 1791. These ten Amendments are called the Bill of Rights. The first Amendment in this Bill of Rights says:

> *"Congress shall make no law respecting an establishment of religion, or prohibiting the free exercise thereof."*

This Amendment guarantees to every citizen the right to believe in his own idea of God and the right to hold different religious beliefs from others. People have the right to think different thoughts, to live in different ways and to believe in different things.

The men who wrote the Constitution represented a cross-section of the religions of the new country—Episcopalians, Congregationalists, Presbyterians, Roman Catholics, Quakers and Methodists. Some of the most important leaders in the fight for religious liberty in America were not members of any particular church, but all had deep personal beliefs in God. These liberal men, varied in their beliefs, established a true freedom to worship in America.

The *Freedom to Worship* series presents stories of outstanding Americans of the nineteenth century, and their different religious beliefs which either were brought to our country or originated here. It tells how a variety of religions produced a variety of people, many of whom contributed to the growth and development of America.

The MORMONS

The Church of Jesus Christ
of Latter-day Saints

WRITTEN AND ILLUSTRATED BY

KATHLEEN ELGIN

With a Foreword by Ray Knell,
President
National Society Sons of the Utah Pioneers

DAVID McKAY COMPANY, Inc.

THE
Freedom to Worship
SERIES

NEW YORK

To R. D.

Contents

Foreword

THE QUESTION WHICH MEMBERS of the Church of Jesus Christ of Latter-Day Saints (Mormons) usually ask in their approach to a religious conversation is: "What do you know about the Mormons? Would you like to know more?" Hundreds of thousands of interested persons respond favorably to this question each year, as the spectacular increase in Church membership attests. There are now approaching three million members of this church.

How a small but enthusiastic band of exiles, opposed and persecuted, grew into a flourishing, world-wide religion and how they helped push back the frontier of the 19th-century America, is one of the historic epochs of modern times. An exciting story, dominated by the devotion, sacrifices and sufferings of the Mormon pioneers, this book is also an account of a religion that combines the needs of everyday life with sacred doctrine and divine revelation.

The author has depicted with deep understanding the role of the Mormons in the settling of the West and the part they played in the development of a unique and dynamic religion.

Ray Knell

President
National Society Sons of the Utah Pioneers

Acknowledgment

My thanks to Earl C. Tingey, Bishop of the Manhattan Ward, for unlocking important doors, and to John Q. Cannon, Coordinator of the Church Information Service in Salt Lake City, who was behind one of them.

—K. E.

"The best and only security for religious liberty in any society is a multiplicity of sects. Where there is such a variety of sects, there cannot be a majority of any one sect to oppress and persecute the rest."

JAMES MADISON

THE MORMONS

There will always be new frontiers to conquer and explore. Today there are the frontiers of the ocean depths and the heights of outer space. Yesterday there was the challenge of another kind of expansion—the opening of the Great American West.

Pioneers of the early 1800's left the relative safety of the eastern United States to explore the mystery that lay beyond the Mississippi. Among these were the Mormons.

· Sustained by their faith and confident in their strength, more than 85,000 Mormons—men, women, and children—pushed westward in search of religious freedom, and to escape persecution. They rode on horseback and muleback, and in wagons. Many walked the thirteen hundred hazardous miles from their Midwest settlements to the Salt Lake valley of Utah. Some three thousand of them toiled and trudged along, pulling and pushing wooden, two-wheeled handcarts, crammed with their belongings, across rivers, through the wilderness and over mountains to their Promised Land. Six thousand dead were left on the trail.

The Mormons

No more self-reliant generation than these early nineteenth century Americans can be found in our history. They knew the power of, and believed in, the dignity of hard work. In spite of persecution and rejection by state and Federal governments, they became loyal Americans. Their contribution to the development of the country was invaluable. Mormons laid out the first route for overland mail service. Later, when the Pony Express was started, the riders used the original way stations and routes of the early Saints.

The Union Pacific Railroad followed closely the old Mormon Trail. So does U.S. Highway 30 today. A team of Mormons, hired by the Central Pacific Railroad, and working under the direction of Ezra Taft Benson, laid the connecting rails of the East and the West at Promontory Point, Utah. They were there when the last spike, the golden one, was driven in on May 10, 1869.

The Saints plowed and seeded hundreds of acres of land on their trails from Illinois to Salt Lake, and beyond—to the California coast. They laid foundations for future settlements; built churches and temples, schools and cities. They sowed so that others might reap. Their strong family ties provided a feeling of security, as necessary today as then.

Every Mormon child hears both in his home and in his Church, stories about the heroism and strength of his ancestors; stories about the building of communities and the Temples at Kirtland, Ohio, and Nauvoo, Illinois, and their ultimate destruction; stories about the incredible migration to Utah; stories of how modern methods of irrigation in the American desert were begun by Mormons. The stories, passed on from generation to generation, tell also of the victims of the winter march across Iowa, and of the persecution and suffering these martyrs endured because of their religious beliefs.

Among the many deserving of recognition and honor, one

14

name stands out—Charles Coulson Rich. Pioneer, leader in the first trek to the Rockies, Rich helped open the frontier to the West. He was instrumental in bringing a remarkably organized and stable government to the wilderness known as the Utah Territory. He devoted his life to the same goals we strive for today—to live peaceably together as a united people, free from fear and want.

CHARLES COULSON RICH

Pioneer and Lawmaker

In 1831, Charles Coulson Rich was twenty-three years old. Six feet, four inches tall, weighing two hundred and twenty pounds, he looked every inch the Western pioneer. He worked his father's six-hundred-acre farm in the summer months, growing wheat and potatoes, and raising cattle. In the winter he taught the small school in Tazewell County, Illinois.

In 1831, Illinois was new country. Land was virgin and cheap. Plots of a hundred acres could be easily acquired, either by purchase at $1.25 an acre, cash or credit, or by "squatting." In 1831, Andrew Jackson, "Old Hickory," was in the White House. Western expansion was one of President Jackson's pet programs. The West *was* opening up; limitless opportunity awaited the brave and the adventurous.

Charles Rich came from a long line of pioneers, breakers of new soil. They had always lived on the ever-shifting frontier, with its hardships, its privations, its dangers. His boyhood playmates were Indians who taught him to hunt and fish.

Charles worked on his father's farm from the time he was old enough to carry a milk pail, or lead the horses while his father pushed the plow. The boy went to the one-room, log cabin district school for three months of the year. He grew up with and in the Illinois Territory, which became the State of Illinois in 1818.

In Rich's twenty-third year, two Mormon elders, missionaries Lyman Wight and John Corrill, came to Tazewell County. Wight was a big, raw-boned man, rough and bold; he lived up to his nickname of the "Wild Ram of the Mountains." Corrill was a very different sort of man. He seemed composed, intellectual and reserved, but inside, just like Lyman Wight, he was on fire with the spirit of a new religion—the Church of Jesus Christ of Latter-day Saints, or the Mormons.

When these men began to preach, and to deliver their earnest message, they created a sensation. People were filled with awe at the thought that, now living in Ohio, not a far way off from their own outpost of civilization, was a young man who, like Moses, had seen and talked face to face with God! They marveled that young Joseph Smith had actually seen the Father and the Son, and that both had spoken to him!

It was said that this young man, now twenty-six years old, and his friend Oliver Cowdery, had organized the new Church just two years before; that young Smith had published a book, the *Book of Mormon*, which he had translated from thin, golden plates found near his father's farm in Palmyra, in western New York State.

The preaching of the two Mormon missionaries made a profound and startling impression on many, including Charles Rich. But with his deliberate and searching nature, he took nearly a year before he reached his decision to become a Latter-day Saint, an LDS.

Three Mormon elders baptized him into the Church in the spring of 1832. After this, young Rich walked the six hundred miles to Ohio to visit Joseph Smith, the Prophet, and founder of the Church. True to Mormon ideal, the new convert preached Mormonism wherever he could along the way. When twenty-four-year-old Charles Rich looked into the kindly eyes of the twenty-seven-year-old Prophet, he thought, "These are the same eyes that have looked upon God!"

He spent days listening to the startling experiences and profound beliefs of Joseph Smith. A close relationship and mutual trust was established between the two young men.

The youthful disciple went back to Illinois determined to devote his life to the cause of the new religion. He had studied intently, not only with the elders who had baptized him but also with Joseph Smith, in long conversations and prayers. Supported by the Bible and the *Book of Mormon*, he preached the doctrine of the Mormon Church, an approach representing a return to the primitive church of early Christianity.

For the next five years, Charles preached the faith whenever he could leave his work on the farm. He rode the rough trails of Illinois on horseback, alone. Always introspective, this quality was deepened in his solitary missions and brought him a new maturity and knowledge of himself and others. He met whites and Indians, trappers, hunters and farmers; good men and bad. Alone he rode into villages and farms; after his first few trips out, his tall frame and easy manner became known throughout the state. Charles believed passionately in the new Church and projected his belief in an earnest, quiet manner that gained many converts for the Latter-day Saints of the Prophet Joseph Smith.

Then, one trail took him through Looking Glass Prairie, where he met twenty-three-year-old Sarah Pea. They were married four months later, in February of 1838. The young couple decided to settle in Missouri. Here a new Mormon community called Far West, headed by Joseph Smith, needed strong and willing hands to help establish this outpost.

Two years before, on a missionary trip with Lyman Wight, Charles had bought forty acres of land in Far West, realizing that some day he would want to settle down in the area where the Prophet would lead. As a wedding present, Charles's father staked his son to another forty acres of good farm land, adjacent to the original land.

From the land, bountiful with water and timber, came the materials to build the couple's home—logs for the cabin, split rails for fencing; ash, oak and fruitwood for simple, sturdy furniture; mud and stone for the fireplace and chimney.

Sarah's father had given her a good riding horse with saddle, bridle, and martingale as a wedding present. Charles had a good horse and rig for driving, and in this they went to meeting every Sunday to hear the Prophet Joseph preach. By their hard work and strengthened by their faith, Sarah and Charles Rich cleared and worked their land and established themselves in the growing Mormon pioneer colony. From then on, for the next forty-five years, Charles was in the center of two important activities—the growth of a great religious movement and the westward expansion of America.

The Mormons

The summer of 1838 passed; rumors reached Charles Rich that trouble was brewing for the Mormons. The settlement in and around Far West had reached a population of fifteen thousand; the Mormons had established their own communal economy and independence. They had the best houses and the best farm lands, and they were coming close to controlling the politics of the state by their vote bloc.

Prejudice against, and jealousy of the Mormons built up to a crescendo of hate. The threats by non-Mormons caused Charles to move his wife, in September, from the outlying farm into the main community of Far West. Both sides, the militant mob forces and the Mormons, in stunned self-defense, armed themselves. Joseph Smith organized a small company; they were under the command of Colonels Hinkle and Wight, and Captains Patten and Rich.

The insistent beating of drums in the public square of Far West awakened her citizens near midnight on October 24, 1838. This prearranged signal, agreed upon in time of danger to the community, brought several hundred men to the square. Hastily dressing, Charles pulled on his heavy boots. Sarah took his rifle from the wall and gave it to him as he ran out the doorway of their cabin.

Captain Rich was among the first to arrive in the square. Exciting news awaited him and the other men. A rabble rouser named Samuel Bogart had led thirty to forty men that morning to Log Creek, just outside Far West. He had threatened two Mormons with death unless they left their homes and the state, and had taken three other Saints as prisoners under the same threat.

Seventy-five men volunteered to rescue the three prisoners and to break up the unruly mob under Bogart. The company of volunteers was placed in charge of Captain Patten, with Captain Charles Rich second in command.

Shortly before one in the morning of the twenty-fifth, a solemn, preoccupied procession moved out of Far West. Only the sound of horses' hoofs on the cold hard ground and the rattling of sabers disturbed the still October night. About ten miles west from the center of town, at a place called Crooked River, the men silently dismounted. They left their horses with a few guards and crept, guns at ready, toward the hanging willows and heavy grasses along the banks of the narrow stream.

The first faint pink and orange tints of dawn showed on the horizon; the grass was slippery with morning dew, and squeaky underfoot. Suddenly a shot cracked the stillness and a young Mormon named O'Banion had seen his last morning.

The Mormons

Fifty yards from the stream, the Mormons fired into the silhouetted trees and grasses. Their fire was immediately returned and volleys were exchanged rapidly and blindly. Four Mormons fell. Patten ordered hand-to-hand combat, and Captain Rich shouted the signal: "God and Liberty!"

Sword in hand he led his men forward. This unexpected action utterly confused the enemy. They fled through the grasses into the water, stumbling along the river bank through the dense branches of the willows, trying to get to the other side and safety. Suddenly one of Bogart's men stopped in his flight, turned, and from behind a tree shot Captain Patten in the abdomen.

Rich, the leader now, ordered his men to continue the chase. He knelt beside his commander to see how serious was his wound and realized that Patten was dying. Rich made him as comfortable as possible, said a few gentle words of prayer for him, and joined his men. Bogart and his company had fled in panic across the river, leaving several wounded men.

Charles and the other Mormons had thought they were going after a mob under the control of the bigot, Samuel Bogart. Actually, the enemy was a company of state militia under *Captain* Samuel Bogart, the same unprincipled man, but with authority given him by the state. When Captain Rich realized he had been in combat against official state forces, he turned over to the state command in Far West all the supplies and ammunition which Bogart and his men had abandoned in their frantic escape from Crooked River.

Rich and Bogart met again later that month. Bogart, now in command of two thousand state militia, was camped just outside of Far West. Captain Rich rode out to neutral territory to return two prisoners from the Crooked River rout. He met Bogart on the field of the encampment and turned over the wounded men. His staff—a flag of truce—still in his hand, Charles wheeled his horse around.

Without warning, Bogart fired at Rich's back—and missed. Charles reined his horse, pulled his pistol and raised it to shoot. But just as quickly he changed his mind, lowered his gun and rode slowly to camp. He gave his reason sometime later: "A friend of mine was a prisoner of Captain Bogart, and the captain might have taken out his revenge on him— if I missed."

The skirmish at Crooked River had been the pretext for bringing out the militia against the Mormons. A false report of Crooked River, given to Governor Boggs of Missouri, caused the governor to issue an order to expel the Mormons from the state.

The report, dated October 24, 1838, said that Captain Bogart and all of his company of fifty to sixty men, except three, had been massacred by Mormons. Three days later, the governor issued his order: "The Mormons must be treated as enemies and must be exterminated or driven from the state, if necessary, for the public good. These outrages are beyond all description."

The Mormon band under Patten and Charles Rich had made their silent march to Crooked River the day *after* the report was given to the governor!

After this, Charles Rich was in grave danger. Saints, in fear of their lives, had gathered together whatever property they could and fled to the border. Mormon leaders had been, or were being rounded up for trial and execution. Property of the Church was being confiscated by the state. Joseph and

Hyrum Smith, along with Lyman Wight and other religious leaders were in jail. Captain Patten was dead. It was rumored that Bogart's bullet had killed Charles Rich.

But it soon became known that Charles was alive; the only Mormon leader still free, he had to get out of Missouri. He left Sarah at one o'clock on a moonless November night, not knowing if they would ever see each other again.

As soon as he reached Illinois territory, Charles sent a fast rider with a message to Sarah's father, to let him know of his own safety and whereabouts, and that his daughter was secure in her Missouri home. Three months later, in the first week of February, 1839, Sarah's father was able to go to Missouri and take Sarah out of the state. They left with just about the only Mormons remaining in Far West; all of their family property was in two wagons. More than two hundred miles on the frozen ground of rough trails, in bitter, stormy Midwest weather faced them before they came to the Mississippi River and crossed over to the safety of Illinois. Within two hours after she arrived, Sarah gave birth to her first-born, Sarah Jane.

For six weeks after little Sarah was born, Sarah's life was in danger; the hardships of the trip had almost taken the two lives. When she recovered, Sarah, Charles, and their baby daughter moved to a place called Commerce. On an acre and a half Charles built another home, hewn from the land, and furnished again with plain furniture which he himself had made. He cut wood for fuel for the coming winter of 1839–40, and here the small family settled. He and Sarah established a happy home again. They had neighbors who shared the dangers, privations, and isolation of the frontier, as well as the rewards of independence and freedom.

Missouri freed Joseph and Hyrum Smith and Lyman Wight and they came to Commerce. The little outpost flourished under the direction of Prophet Joseph Smith. Within a few short years it became the carefully planned city of Nauvoo, a name meaning beautiful in an Indian dialect. Nauvoo was given its City Charter by the Illinois State Legislature. It was the biggest city in Illinois and had the largest body of trained and disciplined soldiers in the West, second only to the United States Army. These soldiers were members of the Nauvoo Legion which Smith had organized to protect the Mormons and to prevent the plunder and bloodshed that had driven them from Missouri. Joseph Smith headed the Legion, Charles Rich was second in command. But on April 29, 1844, Prophet Smith signed an appointment, making Brigadier General Charles Rich commander of the Nauvoo Legion.

The success of Nauvoo, however, was not to last. Once more, fear and jealousy broke out and once more violence took over. In June, 1844, a mob, roused to a fever pitch of hostility, murdered Joseph Smith and his brother Hyrum.

After the death of Joseph Smith, Brigham Young became the Mormon Prophet. For a while, shame over the killing of Joseph and his brother quieted the turmoil of hostile feelings. But then the old prejudice erupted again in Illinois. The State Legislature disbanded the Legion and revoked the Nauvoo City Charter. Illinois, as Missouri had done, decreed that the Saints had to leave the state within six months.

Before leaving Nauvoo, Rich, after long deliberation with himself and Sarah, and with the approval of President Young, decided to enter into "plural marriage." This concept of marriage, which provided for a rapid growth in the Mormon population, had been announced by Joseph Smith, and followed by Brigham Young. Four young women were chosen as Charles's wives, their parents' consent was obtained, and Sarah instructed them in the principle of plural marriage. Four sacred ceremonies were held in the Nauvoo Temple.

These four wives had interesting and divergent backgrounds, but they shared the same idea—to help Charles Rich, to bear his children, and to live together amicably and in the best of morality and taste. The second wife, Eliza Graves, was a small woman, weak in constitution, modest and retiring. She had a solid ancestry in New England and Ireland. Mary Phelps, the third wife, who came from Illinois Territory, was another type of woman. She was resourceful and independent. Sarah Peck, the fourth wife, like the first Sarah, was a large woman, noted for her generosity and kindness. She always gave thirteen eggs to the dozen! Emeline Grove, the fifth of Charles' wives, was also a large woman. Later, in Utah, she obtained a diploma in nursing and practiced this profession for many years.

"Many will think it strange," says the first Mrs. Rich in her *Autobiography*, "that I should consent for my husband, whom I loved as I did my own life and with whom I had lived for years, to take more wives. This I would not have done if I had not believed it to be right in the sight of God, to be a principle of the Gospel, and if I had not believed that those who obeyed the principle of plural marriage would receive a higher glory in the Eternal World."

On the twelfth of February, 1846, eight days after the first wagons had left Nauvoo, Charles, four of his wives and three children crossed over the river to begin the trek westward. Eliza Rich, who gave birth to her first child on the thirteenth, followed a few days later, on one of the return trips made by Charles.

The Riches joined up with the other Mormons who were prepared to make the long journey west. Nine miles north-west of Nauvoo, on the Iowa side of the Mississippi, was Sugar Creek, the starting point for the caravan. The Mormons left there on the twenty-fifth of February; it was twelve degrees below zero. The rough trails were drifted with a new snowfall on top of the winter-packed base. Making camp the first night the men dug away the snow to make places for pallets, as there was no room to sleep in the wagons, chock-full of provisions.

Everyone, even the babies (nine children had been born the first bitter night out of Nauvoo), had to sleep on the frozen ground. Branches of trees were spread out on the snow. Later, as they journeyed, the travelers learned to spread leafed branches on the soft mud, to keep their blankets from becoming altogether unusable. Sarah kept a rag carpet to put down on the branches. She, like the others, did the cooking outside, rain or shine, sometimes on a stove, but more often over a campfire.

Before starting out, the Rich women had made small cakes from dried squash. They carried these cakes in clean white sacks, and after soaking the thin patties in milk, made them into "squash pies."

Each company of ten wagons had a few milk cows; frequently these had to be yoked to the wagons to help pull them through the most difficult places. The hard conditions—rain, cold, mud, damp beds, and lack of proper food—made illness a constant companion on the trail west. When the snow melted in the first weeks of March, the animals plowed through a foot of mud that the thaw had made. Mud, and more mud—there seemed to be no end to the mud. It rained incessantly through March and April. Many times the wagons had to be unloaded and then pulled, empty, over the worst places.

The companies made about two miles a day; they did not move on Sundays. Some week days, too, they did not move— because of sickness, because the men had to hunt for food, because they stopped to sow fields, but most of all, because of the weather. Sometimes they could go only a half a mile a day. From Nauvoo west there were no roads, just wilderness broken through by the youngest and strongest men who had gone ahead to clear the trail.

The Mormons

About midway between the Mississippi and Missouri rivers, on the Middle Thompson River, was a place the Mormons called Mount Pisgah, after the mountain ridge of ancient Palestine, from whose summit Moses viewed the Promised Land. One hundred seventy-two miles from Nauvoo, the broad plateau overlooks the flat prairie of Iowa.

The Mormon westward migration was an organized movement. The pioneers were divided into companies, each with its own appointed captain. By the first of June, 1846, almost a thousand wagons had met at Mount Pisgah. Every family was supposed to have started from Nauvoo with enough supplies for three months. Charles Rich hadn't expected even to go in the first company; but Brigham Young had asked him to lead it.

He had not been properly supplied when they left Nauvoo; so along the way through Iowa, he did whatever work he could find. He was not the only man in that position. Along the trail, at isolated farms and in the six cabin beginnings of towns, the men worked for provisions necessary for their families to continue. At a place called Reed's Creek, for example, Charles and his men cleared ten acres of land; he made shingles, he shoed horses, mules and cattle. At still another time he cleared other land and was paid twenty-three bushels of corn, which went into the rear storage of the family wagons.

The scout company, under the leadership of Brigham Young, had reached Mount Pisgah only four days before. But already they had plowed acres of land, fenced it, and put it to seed! Young, before he left Mount Pisgah, appointed three men to manage the Mormon colony that was to stay until they were ready to move on. The three were William Huntington, Ezra Taft Benson, and Charles Rich.

The Mormon pioneers built log cabins on Mount Pisgah. In early August, as autumn approached, they moved down to the river's edge where they could be close to wood and water. The cabins on the hill had earth for floors and roofs; the ones on the river had both floors and roofs of the bark of the easily peeled oak tree. Often these cabins were lighted by candles stuck into hollowed turnips, nailed to the walls.

Settling near the river meant living with mosquitoes; the third week in August, yellow fever struck the settlement at Mount Pisgah. During the long weeks of an unusually hot September, there were more sick people than well. The dead lay for three or four days before there were enough recovered persons to bury them. When they were buried, it was often without a coffin, because there was not enough lumber. More than one widow had a wagon bed sawed up and made into a casket for her husband. The loss of so many men was a basic and practical reason for plural marriages; the widows and children needed the strength and protection of the Mormon men who survived, on the trail and after they arrived in Salt Lake.

William Huntington died; Ezra Taft Benson was made an apostle of the Church; Charles Rich became president of the Mount Pisgah settlement. He worked day and night, nursing the sick, burying the dead, until yellow fever struck him. For fifteen days he lay between life and death. This giant of a man wasted away to a hundred and sixty pounds. At last he defeated the fever—he had a people to lead to their Promised Land.

But there was not only sickness and poverty in the ten months the Riches were at Mount Pisgah. When the fever had gone, during the long months of recovery, the men worked at making barrels, tubs, churns, baskets, and other practical articles for market in the non-Mormon farms and settlements of Iowa and beyond. The income from this labor was shared by all, not just the workers but the many needy who could not participate.

In March, 1847, after he had recovered fully, Charles, with his large family of five wives and six children, went to Winter Quarters, the settlement where the main body of Mormons had spent the winter. Winter Quarters was on the west side of the Missouri, and is now the city of Omaha, Nebraska. In Winter Quarters, Charles married his sixth wife, the strikingly beautiful Harriet Sargent.

Three months later, the Saints left Winter Quarters, on the twenty-first of June. The first company of two thousand persons was divided into three groups; Rich led one. He was also in command of the Artillery Division, with military equipment to protect the company going through a wilderness of wild animals and Indians.

For safety and protection at night, Rich ordered the wagons drawn up to form a circle. The front wheels of one wagon were interlocked with the back wheels of the next. This formed a huge corral for the cattle and horses, and the tents were pitched on the outside.

Rich led this first company on the trail, after Brigham Young's scouts, and so he had not the benefit of others' experience of directing a large group as had later companies. The wives of Charles Rich kept diaries which give first-hand accounts of this Mormon venture. Sarah Rich divided the westward trail into three parts—the buffalo, the prairie dog, and the mountain region.

FROM THE DIARY OF SARAH RICH

July, 1847:

The company don't travel fast enough through the buffalo country—the men folk all want to kill a buffalo. The meat is made into "jerked beef." The men fixed up a scaffold of willows; the meat was then cut into thin slices and spread out to dry. Fires were made underneath. When one side was dried, the meat was turned over till it was dry.

Buffalo meat is the sweetest I ever tasted. It made the children fat. It was a grand sight to see thousands of these animals racing across the prairie; the wagons seemed to frighten them; and it caused us to fear that they might attack us.

The Mormons

August, 1847:

After we got through with the buffalos, we came to the land of the prairie dogs. The whole country was alive with them. They lived in holes in the ground, and would fill the air with their barking all night long. They were about the size of puppies, very handsome, only with more fur than hair. They would sit by their holes, and stick out their heads and bark. Some of the men tried vainly to catch them alive for pets. In one place there were so many of them that it was called "Dog Town."

FROM THE DIARY OF MARY RICH

August, 1847:

There were hundreds of Indians along the way all the time we were traveling up the Platte River. They were very cunning. We had to watch them very closely, to see that they did not steal everything we had. They would shoot arrows into our cattle and sheep. So we found it took more hands to herd the cattle and drive the wagons than we had anticipated.

Mr. Rich thought he would have to hire two more boys or men to drive two of the wagons, but there was one of the wives besides myself who had no children. So we volunteered to drive until we got to the valley. He did not think we could, but we persuaded him to try us one day, and see. We did so well that we had our own teams every day after that, until we arrived in the valley.

We did not grieve or mourn over the journey; we had some very nice times, when the roads were not so bad. We would make the mountains ring with our songs, and sometimes the company got together in a dance of an evening on the grass. We rejoiced, instead of mourning, that we were going to the Rocky Mountains, where we would be free to live our religion, and be acknowledged as wives.

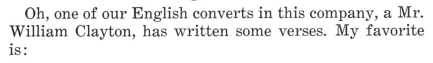

Oh, one of our English converts in this company, a Mr. William Clayton, has written some verses. My favorite is:

> *Come, come ye Saints, no toil nor labor fear,*
> *But with joy wend your way;*
> *Tho' hard to you this journey may appear,*
> *Grace shall be as your day.*
> *'Tis better far for us to strive*
> *Our useless cares from us to drive;*
> *Do this, and joy your hearts will swell—*
> *All is well! All is well!*

Besides, we felt that we wanted to do everything in our power to help out Mr. Rich, as his children were small and he needed our aid. I had never had very good health, until I started on that trip. And then I got to feeling so well that I felt it was a pleasure to take hold and do something.

When we arrived in Emigration Canyon, the longest place on my dress was just a little below my knees. I had walked over the brush driving my team, to keep them in the road, and could not stop to untangle my dress when it got fastened, but had to walk on, leaving part of my dress behind.

Emeline and Mary Rich had led their teams, walking eleven hundred miles to the valley. One hundred and three days after leaving Winter Quarters, on October 2, 1847, Charles Rich, at the head of his company, arrived at the Salt Lake valley. Brigham Young's scout company was already established; more than three hundred and seventy-five people were in the valley. The men were mostly hand-picked for repairing wagons, shoeing horses and mules, building bridges and houses, innovating irrigation systems, planting and harvesting. Salt Lake valley was eleven hundred miles from the nearest settlement to the east, and eight hundred miles from the nearest one to the west.

FROM THE DIARY OF EMELINE RICH

October 1, 1847:

Very scantily clad and poorly fed, as we were, we truly had a hard journey, and were glad when we saw before us the Salt Lake valley, although a barren desert at that time and without inhabitants.

The Mormons

The Saints faced a fifty-fifty chance of survival. There would be no provisions coming in; there would be no real harvest before the tough intermountain winter. The Mormons were in the middle of what was marked on all maps at that time as the Great American Desert. They were surrounded by Indians—the Blackfeet, the Crows, and the Bannocks.

Charles Rich was then thirty-eight. He was, after President Brigham Young, the main planner of the Salt Lake settlement. He began the planting in the Big Field; he sent men to the west coast for work animals, beef cattle, and cows. He negotiated with traders and trappers in the Salt Lake territory, which was then Mexican, for exchange of goods. He dealt with the Indians, honestly and fairly, as he had dealt with other people all of his life, and established friendly relations with them.

He helped to set up a government which was equitable to all, yet was capable of stern discipline and punishing those who would not cooperate in building the community.

A ten-acre plot was set apart as Temple Square. On this land the imposing Salt Lake Temple would one day rise. The settlers built a square fort; the east side was a row of log cabins, roofed with brush and mud, slanting inward; the windows and doors faced the inside of the fort. The walls were mud.

But for many of the first Mormons in the valley, their initial homes were simply tents or their wagon beds.

From the Diary of Sarah Rich

October 14, 1847:

General Rich and his men fixed up a tent as comfortably as they could for us women to cook and eat in. We had a little sheet-iron stove to cook on; our wagon boxes were our bedrooms. In this way we spent the first three or four weeks, till the men could go to the canyon for logs.

November 27, 1847:

Mr. Rich and his teamsters went to work and, by hand, sawed or split logs, and built us some good rooms in the north fort. [Two other forts had been built to accommodate newcomers.] We thought they were very nice, for the logs had been fitted together so well that the inside walls were smooth and even. So when we moved into our new home, we felt as though we were to be very comfortable. The cabins just plain got dark at night. But then we fixed up what everyone calls a "bitch-wick," because its flicker is so unsteady. Tallow is poured into a saucer, and a narrow strip of cloth put in for a wick.

August, 1848:

Between October, 1847, when we arrived in the valley, and this August, we were put on rations—three ounces of breadstuff a day to each person. We had to dig roots, what the Indians called sego. [The roots of the sego lily, now the state flower of Utah.] They are bitter, but these answer for potatoes, when cooked; and when we had milk to make gravy with, they were very nice. There were thistles growing in the valley, which made good greens; they were quite a help to us in those times.

SEGO LILY

THISTLE

FROM THE DIARY OF MARY RICH

August, 1848:

During that first winter (1847–48) we had a hard time, as provisions were short, and our family was large. We had cows, some sheep, and two horses; but we had no meat, other than some of the cattle that we had worked on the road, which were really not fit to eat. We were obliged to kill some, nevertheless, in order to subsist and make our provisions hold out.

CACTUS

Rich was made one of the twelve Apostles * of the Church at the age of forty; he was also president of the Salt Lake Stake.* To establish the Mormon Church west of the Salt Lake valley, and particularly in California, Brigham Young sent Charles Rich on still another pioneer expedition.

Rich led to the coast a group of about twenty-five missionaries, five of whom were going on to the Society Islands in the South Pacific! They went with two other groups, one of five hundred, the other of twenty, bound for the gold fields in the Sacramento Valley of California; gold had been discovered not long after the Latter-day Saints pioneers reached the valleys of the mountains.

They expected to go south to the Little Salt Lake valley where they could pick up the Old Spanish Trail. It ran from the valley southwest to the Cajon Pass in the Sierra Nevadas. The Spanish Trail was a trail, not a road. No wagon had ever gone over it until then. The Rich wagon, pulled by six oxen, had on it an odometer, for measuring distance, attached to a wheel. Every ten miles they stopped, and hammered a stake

* See chart on Church organization, page 86.

into the ground, marking the mileage for those who would follow. The stakes were lettered *C. C. Rich*, and the distance marked from the Great Salt Lake valley was the first marking of distance in the Southwest.

The three groups had left a day or two apart on different schedules but they met at Minersville, in the Sevier valley. Captain Smith, leader of the five hundred gold seekers, wanted to take a new trail to the coast—Walker's Cut-Off. The majority of the men decided to take the cut-off instead of the Spanish Trail, because it would bring them up the coast nearer to Sacramento, save hundreds of miles, and get them to the gold fields more quickly. Against Rich's better judgment, they started out.

The five hundred and forty-five men left the Spanish Trail and struck out due west for the cut-off. For the first few days, the weather was good, water and grass plentiful, and they met no unfriendly Indians. Then they hit the mountains. Traveling down canyon on a two-foot-wide trail, there were places where one false step would have meant plunging hundreds of feet down the rock precipice.

From that day on, the Mormons ran into nothing but trouble. It stormed and rained for days. The trail was hazardous and difficult. The greedy gold hunters threatened to kill the others if their food supply ran out. (This had been done before on the westward trail.)

Finally Rich realized that they were lost in the Sierras. He ordered the men who would follow him back to the Spanish Trail. His company of twenty-five missionaries, and four of the other groups, left what was called Division Springs, after filling their canteens with good drinking water. General Rich led the company in a southwest direction heading for the Spanish Trail. Within two days they hit good grass and water, and after making good time of about fifteen miles a day, within a week found the intersection of the Muddy River and the Spanish Trail.

Later, twelve men who had decided to leave the big group of five hundred straggled into the Mormon camp. A terrible fate awaited those gold seekers of '49 who persisted in getting to the gold diggings by the Walker Cut-Off. Of the five hundred who left Utah, only fifteen survived. One by one they dropped by the non-existent trail called the cut-off, and gave a name to the valley through which they had traveled. They perished from hunger and thirst—in Death Valley.

The Mormons under Rich stayed at the Muddy only long enough to shoe their horses and mules, and started out for the coast again. Sixty-five days after leaving the Salt Lake valley, Rich arrived at the Chino Ranch in the San Bernardino Valley. Then on January 18, Rich took the missionaries in his company up the coast to San Francisco. Brigham Young had instructed him to begin collecting tithes and donations, to receive money for the Perpetual Fund for poor Saints, and to preach Mormon philosophy and belief. By July, he had collected more than four thousand dollars, and preached at every opportunity.

Early in September, 1850, Rich began his return trip to the Salt Lake valley. He rode a pony, and led a mule which carried a pack of food, cooking utensils, and his bedroll. Fifty-one men returning to Salt Lake were in the group he headed. On October 12, he reported to Brigham Young, and gave him the collected money, even before seeing his families. Young asked him to return to California in the spring, to start a Mormon settlement in San Bernardino.

On the sixteenth of March, 1851, Rich led a 150-wagon company out of the valley. There were four hundred and thirty-seven people, 588 oxen, 336 cows, 21 young stock, 107 horses, and 52 mules.

This journey, which took almost three months [today's flight time is one hour!], was a hard one. The wagon train slowly creaked its way over the mountains east of the Muddy. All of the women had to walk, some of them carrying their children. Rich's company traveled in groups of ten wagons, each group under a captain, in the typical Mormon way. The trail was rocky—grass and water were very scarce—the kegs of drinking water for human beings and animals were often empty.

They had to cross four deserts—cattle and oxen were left along the trail—just too weak to go on without water. Those animals that survived did so because the men carried water back to them in kegs and cans and buckets. In some places they had to lower the wagons over the steep cliffs with ropes, to make it over the mountains.

Charles Rich finally arrived at Cajon Pass, with no sickness or death in his large group of men, women, and children. They camped in several places, about half a mile apart, to give the cattle plenty of grazing land. The hills were covered with wild oats and mustard, and the valley with luxuriant grass. Rich had gone ahead and staked out the places for their camps in a sycamore grove. He went on to the Chino ranch and bought a large supply of flour and bacon.

The Saints camped at Sycamore Grove from June through September, 1851, just twelve miles northwest of San Bernardino. Rich negotiated with the Lugo brothers—José Maria, José del Carmen, and Vincente—for the 35,500-acre tract of land known as the Rancho del San Bernardino. He settled at a price of $2.17 an acre, a total cost of $77,500, to be paid by the Saints in bi-yearly installments. The bargain was made on September 22, 1851.

About the first of October Rich moved camp out to the ranch and began building for winter quarters. As in the past, very quickly there were substantial homes, a protective fort, and a Big Field—two thousand acres—plowed and planted. In April, they raised their "bowery," and began school classes and religious programs.

A wagon road was completed to the dense forests of pine, hemlock, and redwood which covered the surrounding mountains. Another year and the building of a sawmill to work the timber was engineered by Mormon craftsmen.

Charles Rich, the first mayor of San Bernardino, managed the rapid growth of this Mormon outpost. During the years from 1853 to 1857, another mill was built, an additional two thousand acres were added to the cultivated area of the valley. Fruit trees were planted; a vineyard was begun by the planting of fifty thousand vines.

Apostle Rich spent eight strenuous years in traveling... Salt Lake... San Bernardino... San Francisco. In the spring of 1860 he was sent by Brigham Young to England. In the latter part of June, Rich, with ten other missionaries, sailed from New York on the steamboat *Edinburgh*. Thirteen days later they landed in Liverpool.

During the next two years he traveled through England, Wales, Scotland, Ireland, Italy, France, Switzerland, and the Scandinavian countries. He preached the faith of Mormonism and gained many, many converts, some of whom migrated to America, to Utah and the Southwest.

When he returned to the Salt Lake valley, Rich was sent to set up the communities of the Bear Lake valley in northern Utah. There he immediately established a good relationship with the Shoshone and Bannock Indians. As a matter of fact, there were about three hundred of them baptized into the Church, and the Indian chiefs called Rich the "Big White Chief." Charles Rich was the founder of this great commonwealth of twenty-three towns in one of the most prosperous sections of present-day Utah and Idaho. And among the Mormons, no members of the community were more respected than Rich's own family; he had about fifty children in all, and all of them were good citizens.

During the years following the settlement of Bear Lake, he devoted his life to the growth of the Territory of Utah. The early pioneers knew nothing of party politics; they just knew that good laws had to be made. Charles Rich from Bear Valley, or Rich County, was perhaps the ablest of these lawmakers. During those years, until his illness in 1880, he spoke in the legislature for four different counties, and helped lay the foundations for law and order in the Southwest.

Utah today reflects the early wisdom of men like Charles Rich; her standards of education and social service are unique in the country. Rich brought the best qualities of a man and his religion to the growth of America.

SPUR

The Beginning of
THE MORMONS

Joseph Smith was fourteen that spring morning when he went into the beautiful woods of his father's farm in Palmyra, in upstate New York. He went to seek an answer to a profound question about God. Was He really there, and could He express His thoughts on the turmoil about religion existing in the minds of the American people in the 1820's?

For the first time in his life young Smith tried to pray aloud. Immediately, he was overcome by a power he felt was trying to destroy him.

He wrote later, in a detailed diary, "Just at this moment of great alarm, I saw a pillar of light exactly over my head, above the brightness of the sun, which descended gradually until it fell upon me.

"It no sooner appeared than I found myself delivered from the enemy which held me bound. When the light rested on me I saw two Personages,* whose brightness and glory defy all

* God and His Son, Jesus Christ.

56

description, standing above me in the air. One of them spake unto me, calling me by name and said, pointing to the other, *This is My Beloved Son. Hear Him!*"

Joseph was known as an intelligent and honest young man, but most of the people who heard his story had great doubts. Really! God had not revealed himself for almost eighteen hundred years! Would He do so now? And to a teenage farm boy?

Smith's diary continues: "I had actually seen a light, and in the midst of that light I saw two Personages, and they did in reality speak to me; and though I was hated and persecuted for saying that I had seen a vision, yet it was true; and while they were persecuting me, reviling me, and speaking all manner of evil against me falsely for so saying, I was led to say in my heart: Why persecute me for telling the truth? I have actually seen a vision; and who am I that I can withstand God, or why does the world think to make me deny what I have actually seen? For I had seen a vision; I knew it, and I knew that God knew it, and I could not deny it, neither dared I do it..."

Four years later, on the night of the twenty-first of September, 1823, he wrote: "After I had retired to my bed for the night, I betook myself to prayer and supplication to Almighty God for forgiveness of all my sins and follies, and also for a manifestation to me, that I might know of my state and standing before Him; for I had full confidence in obtaining a divine manifestation, as I had previously had one."

Shortly afterwards, a heavenly being who called himself Moroni, the angel Moroni, son of Mormon, appeared before Joseph. He told him that God had a great work for him to do. Moroni said that in a nearby hill, Cumorah, were thin gold plates, engraved in ancient but decipherable language. Joseph's task was to translate these plates and to pass on the Gospel message from God to the people, to reestablish the fundamental Church.

Joseph found the gold plates in a stone box, in the side of Cumorah Hill. Their protective burial place was covered by a rounded stone lid. But Moroni would not let him take the plates then; he had to return to Cumorah each year, for four years, to receive instruction and to learn "how and in what manner His (God's) kingdom was to be conducted in the last days."

The young prophet, after his indoctrination period was over, took the golden plates from Cumorah. His friend Oliver Cowdery, a schoolteacher, recorded in longhand as Joseph translated, under the inspiration of God, the story. In three months time, the work was done, and the manuscript was published as the *Book of Mormon* in 1830.

Baptism for the forgiveness of sins was mentioned many times in the *Book of Mormon*. During the translation, Joseph Smith and Oliver Cowdery went to the banks of the Susquehanna River, to seek an answer or further explanation of baptism from the Lord.

Facsimile of a portion of the gold plates

The Mormons

While we were thus employed, praying and calling upon the Lord, a messenger from heaven descended in a cloud of light, and having laid his hands upon us, he ordained us, saying:

"Upon you, my fellow servants, in the name of Messiah, I confer the Priesthood of Aaron, which holds the keys of the ministering of Angels, and of the gospel of repentence, and of baptism by immersion for the remission of sins . . ."

He said that this Aaronic Priesthood had not the power of laying on hands for the gift of the Holy Ghost, but that this should be conferred on us hereafter; and he commanded us to go and be baptized, and gave us directions that I should baptize Oliver Cowdery, and afterwards he should baptize me.

Accordingly we went and were baptized. I baptized him first, and afterwards he baptized me—after which I laid my hands upon his head and ordained him to the Aaronic Priesthood, and afterwards he laid his hands on me and ordained me to the Priesthood—for so we were commanded.

The messenger who visited us on this occasion and conferred this Priesthood upon us, said that his name was John, the same that is called John the Baptist in the New Testament, and that he acted under the direction of Peter, James and John, who held the keys of the Melchizedek Priesthood, which Priesthood, he said, would in due time be conferred on us . . .

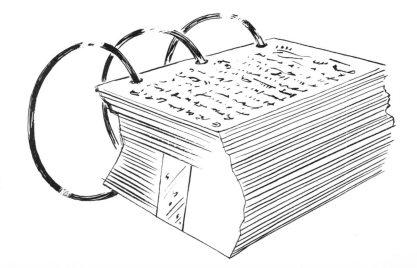

Gold plates
from Comorah Hill

And then by revelation Joseph was instructed that the time had come to organize the true Church. On April 6, 1830, ten years after Joseph Smith had gone into the farm woods, a group of six young men met in a log house in Fayette, New York. New York State laws required six signatures on the Articles of Incorporation, so the papers bore the names of Joseph Smith, his brother Hyrum, David Whitmer, Oliver Cowdery, Peter Whitmer, Jr., and Samuel Smith.

Joseph, then the Prophet, was twenty-four years old; the others were from twenty-one to thirty. The next Sunday the first public announcement and speaking were given. Missionaries were sent out to England within weeks of the Church organization.

The Church moved west with the country, to Ohio and then to what was the western boundary of the United States, Missouri. Joseph Smith believed that eventually the Saints would go all the way west to their promised land of freedom and security. He turned out to be right. For the old settlers in Missouri mistrusted the beliefs and doctrines of the newcomers and feared their unity of purpose, sensing the growth of a solid political bloc.

By order of the governor, the Saints were driven out of the state, to seek sanctuary in Illinois. Smith obtained about a hundred acres in a wilderness called Commerce. A charter for a new city, Nauvoo, had been granted by the Illinois State Legislature (Abraham Lincoln was one who voted for it), and Nauvoo became the largest city in Illinois.

But, as the Prophet had predicted, the same ugly reactions to the Saints developed in Illinois...fear, mistrust, and jealousy. Joseph Smith wrote in his diary on February 20, 1844:

"I instructed the twelve Apostles to send out a delegation and investigate the locations of California and Oregon, and hunt out a good location, where we can remove to after the

Temple is completed, and where we can build a city in a day, and have a government of our own, get up into the mountains, where the devil cannot dig us out, and live in a healthful climate, where we can live as old as we have a mind to... there is a light in the west."

But the storm brewing over Nauvoo developed before scouts could be sent west. Joseph Smith and his brother Hyrum were arrested; the bigots who opposed them believed that the death of the Prophet would be the end of the Mormon Church.

Smith said, "I am going like a lamb to the slaughter; but I am calm as a summer's morning; I have a conscience void of offense towards God, and towards all men. I shall die innocent, and it shall yet be said of me—he was murdered in cold blood."

On the twenty-seventh of June, 1844, a mob broke into the red sandstone jail in Carthage. Hyrum was shot and died instantly. Joseph, mortally wounded by two shots, threw himself from the window in a desperate leap.

His martyrdom did not end the Church as his enemies had hoped. The Council of Twelve Apostles, with Brigham Young as President, took over. Neither did Smith's martyrdom end the prejudice against the Mormons. Nauvoo's city charter was taken away by the legislature; Illinois, as Missouri had done, demanded that the Mormons get out of the state... they gave them six months.

So began another exodus, this time as Joseph Smith had foretold, west to the Rocky Mountains, thirteen hundred miles! The pioneer trail of John Fremont led through the barely settled Iowa Territory, into Indian country. The Omahas, the Sioux, and the Utes ruled the thousand miles beyond.

The first of the Mormon exiles crossed the Mississippi on February 4, 1846. Wagons were ferried across on crude paddle wheel barges day and night; then the mile-wide river froze solidly and for about ten days wagons crossed on the ice. The camp on the west side of the river based at Sugar Creek and soon became organized for the journey west. Progress was slow through the snows of winter and the mud and rain of spring. During the summer hundreds of acres along the trail were plowed and planted, and the endless line of wagons moved towards the Rockies. Some who followed cultivated; others reaped. "Plant that others may harvest!" became the watchword.

The United States was involved in an unfortunate war with Mexico. In late June, the government asked the Mormons, in a "Circular to the Mormons," to furnish five hundred volunteers to join the army in the march to California. Brigham Young saw two things in this—a chance to prove to America that Mormons were loyal citizens, and that filling the quota would take the best men. This left families crossing the plains without fathers and older sons.

Young decided, and five hundred Mormons formed the battalion. Their march through Kansas and the virgin territory of what is now New Mexico, Arizona, and California was the longest infantry march in history. Almost all of the men eventually came back to their families in the Salt Lake valley.

In October about fifteen thousand people with three thousand wagons and thirty thousand head of cattle, many horses, oxen, and sheep had made it to the Missouri River. This place was called Winter Quarters and it was there that most of the Mormon pioneers spent the winter of 1846–47. About a thousand crude cabins and dugouts (caves in the side of a hill, covered over by a roof) lined the banks of the river.

It was rough. An epidemic of "black canker," totally inadequate food, clothing, and shelter, left six hundred in a graveyard near what is now Omaha, Nebraska.

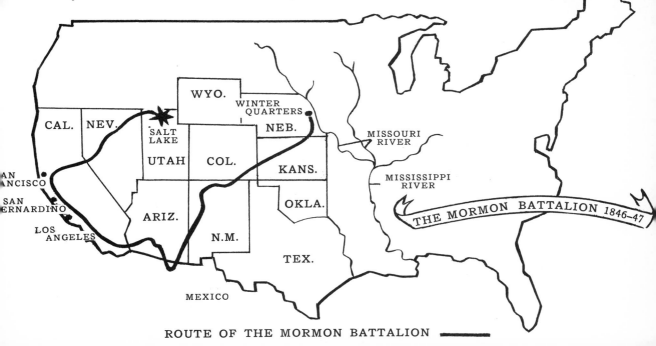

ROUTE OF THE MORMON BATTALION ━━━━

Brigham Young and the Twelve Apostles again headed west in the spring. On July 24, these pioneers came into the valley of the Great Salt Lake. The vast valley was surrounded by mountains, except on the north; some of the highest were capped by snow. The waters of Great Salt Lake glistened in the sun. Young turned to his small group of advance scouts, as they stood on Ensign Peak, overlooking the valley. These men raised the American flag (in Mexican territory!) at the summit of the rounded knoll. The leader commanded, "Now, brethren, organize your exploring parties so as to be safe from the Indians; go and explore where you will, and you will come back here every time and say this is the right place. *This is the place!*"

He later wrote: "In the days of Joseph, we have sat many hours at a time conversing about this very country ... I do not wish men to understand that I had anything to do with our being moved here; that was the providence of the Almighty, it was the power of God ... I never could have devised such a plan ..."

The Mormons had arrived at the Promised Land; they began to make it theirs within hours. While the women prepared for a stationary and permanent home, after months on the move, the men prepared the land for crops. In this part of the valley, the ground was hard, dry and stubborn; plows were broken during the first few days. The Mormons dammed the streams flowing from the mountains, flooded the land being plowed, and began modern irrigation in America.

Their valley it was. The date of their arrival, July 24, is celebrated annually, and is just as important a date to Mormons as is the Fourth of July. Utah, the land of the Mormons, took its name from the Ute tribe of Indians.

These dedicated people laid out the plan for the city; it was plotted into ten acre squares, with wide streets, so that ox-teams could easily turn around. They established schools, and beyond the plotted area were the fenced fields and gardens. Brigham Young selected the site for the future Salt Lake Temple; they built log and adobe houses, as well as a ten acre fort of the same log and adobe.

Then Young led a company back to Winter Quarters to bring new, eager pioneers along the trail to the valley. When they arrived in the spring, they found that five thousand acres were plowed and seeded with wheat. The valley *was* theirs.

But misfortune had not completely left the Mormons. As the wheat was close to harvesting, hordes of destructive crickets invaded the promising crop. Thousands and thousands of the hopping, crawling insects blackened the fields. With long antennae and powerful hind legs they swarmed over the tender young plants, eating them down to the fur-rows. The Mormons beat the fields with wet blankets, sticks, barrel staves, anything, but they could not stop them. As a last resort they opened the irrigation ditches. By the millions the crickets came on.

The Mormons

The Saints at last knelt in the fields and prayed. The sky blackened with still another threat—screeching sea gulls from the lake. But instead of helping destroy the crops, the gulls swooped down and devoured the crickets by the beakful. Returning to the lake time and time again, to drop those they could not eat, the gulls saved the crop. Today the sea gull is the state bird of Utah.

In Salt Lake City's Temple Square is a tall monument, two bronze gulls atop it, erected in honor "of the mercy of God to the Mormon pioneers."

Between 1847, when the first company came into the valley, and the joining of the east-west railroad in 1869, more than eighty-five thousand immigrants trekked across the country. About three thousand, mostly immigrants from England, pushed handcarts all the way. These handcarts allowed just forty pounds of goods to a person. The width of the cart axle matched that of wagon tracks, making it possible to travel in the ruts left by the wagons of preceding pioneers. The body

of the cart was seven feet long and one-and-a-half feet deep. They averaged twelve to fourteen miles a day, some doing twenty, but on some bad days, they made only three or four miles.

The trail west was punishing; shallow graves marked it. Two handcart companies (for the trek was well organized and not a matter of one or two carts starting out alone), which left Iowa City late in the season, lost over two hundred people, more than one out of five, to the early blizzards and freezing weather.

Of the thousands who came to Utah and the coast, some several hundred arrived by ship, and not by wagon or handcart. Two hundred and thirty-eight men, women, and children sailed on the *Brooklyn* from New York in February of 1846. They anchored in the harbor of Yerba Buena (San Francisco) nearly six months later; ten died during that voyage. Twenty Mormons from the ship founded the first known agricultural colony in the San Joaquin valley and planted the first wheat. They irrigated crops by the pole and bucket method, and operated sawmills.

The Salt Lake Mormons, only three years after reaching Utah, founded the University of Deseret, first university west of the Mississippi.

The Mormon colonizers contributed to the founding not only of Utah, but also of Arizona, California, Colorado, Idaho, Montana, Nevada, Wyoming, northern Mexico, and western Canada.

Their initial pioneer efforts and accomplishments have magnified and grown over the years to include such social responsibilities as welfare programs, Church operated farms, ranches and hospitals, schools and universities.

73

WHEAT

QUESTIONS
&
ANSWERS

*Sea gull monument
on Temple Square,
Salt Lake City*

What Is the Book of Mormon?

It contains some of the sacred scriptures of the Mormon Church, recording the history of prophets and peoples, the Nephites, who were led by divine power from Asia to the American continent about 600 B.C. Mormon was one of those prophets, as well as a warrior and historian.

The book was translated from thin gold plates by Joseph Smith, founder of the Church of Jesus Christ of Latter-day Saints. It was first published in 1830. The *Book of Mormon* is used together with the Holy Bible in prayer and worship.

Why Are Latter-Day Saints Called Mormons?

Mormon is a nickname for a member of the Church of Jesus Christ of Latter-day Saints. Most prefer to be called Saints, and use the initials LDS.

WHAT IS THE BELIEF OF A MORMON?

Perhaps the best answer to this is to read the "Articles of Faith," written by Joseph Smith, the founder of the Church:

THE GODHEAD: 1. We believe in God, the Eternal Father, and in His Son, Jesus Christ, and in the Holy Ghost.

RESPONSIBILITY FOR SIN: 2. We believe that men will be punished for their own sins, and not for Adam's transgression.

SALVATION: 3. We believe that through the Atonement of Christ, all mankind may be saved, by obedience to the laws and ordinances of the Gospel.

FIRST PRINCIPLES: 4. We believe that the first principles and ordinances of the Gospel are: first, Faith in the Lord Jesus Christ; second, Repentance; third, Baptism by immersion for the remission of sins; fourth, Laying on of hands for the gift of the Holy Ghost.

AUTHORITY: 5. We believe that a man must be called of God, by prophecy, and by the laying on of hands, by those who are in authority to preach the Gospel and administer in the ordinances thereof.

ORGANIZATION: 6. We believe in the same organization that existed in the Primitive Church: viz., apostles, prophets, pastors, teachers, evangelists, etc.

SPIRITUAL GIFTS: 7. We believe in the gift of tongues, prophecy, revelation, visions, healing, interpretation of tongues, etc.

SCRIPTURES: 8. We believe the Bible to be the word of God as far as it is translated correctly; we also believe the *Book of Mormon* to be the word of God.

REVELATION: 9. We believe all that God has revealed, all that He does now reveal, and we believe that He will yet reveal many great and important things pertaining to the Kingdom of God.

CHRIST'S REIGN ON EARTH: 10. We believe in the literal gathering of Israel and in the restoration of the Ten Tribes; that Zion will be built upon this (the American) continent; that Christ will reign personally upon the earth; and that the earth will be renewed and receive its paradisiacal glory.

FREEDOM: 11. We claim the privilege of worshiping Almighty God according to the dictates of our own conscience, and allow all men the same privilege, let them worship how, where, or what they may.

OBEDIENCE TO LAW: 12. We believe in being subject to kings, presidents, rulers, and magistrates, in obeying, honoring, and sustaining the law.

SEARCH FOR TRUTH: THE GOOD LIFE: 13. We believe in being honest, true, chaste, benevolent, virtuous, and in doing good to all men; indeed, we may say that we follow the admonition of Paul. We believe all things, we hope all things, we have endured many things, and hope to be able to endure all things. If there is anything virtuous, lovely, or of good report or praiseworthy, we seek after those things.

ARE THEY PROTESTANTS?

The Church of Jesus Christ of Latter-day Saints is not "protestant." It is the "restored" Church, begun anew by the appearance of God and His Son, Jesus Christ, to Joseph Smith, reestablishing the same principles and organization which He brought to the earth two thousand years ago.

DID THEY PRACTICE POLYGAMY?

The doctrine of polygamy or "plural marriage," as it was called, was based upon a vision of Joseph Smith in 1843, and announced formally by Brigham Young in 1852. The Mormons of the 19th century entered into plural marriage in the firm belief that it was divinely ordained, as it had been in Biblical times.

Polygamy was practiced by a minority of the Mormons. In 1890, the fourth President of the Church, Wilford Woodruff, revoked the practice, and today the penalty for plural marriage is excommunication.

WHY ARE NON-MORMONS CALLED GENTILES?

Except for Jews, all non-Mormons are referred to as Gentiles, simply meaning those of non-Mormon faith, as to Jews all non-Jews are Gentiles.

WHY ARE THE LEADERS CALLED APOSTLES?

Prophet Joseph Smith wrote, "We believe in the same organization that existed in the Primitive Church." Jesus had set the pattern: "And He ordained twelve, that they should be with Him, and that He might send them forth to preach." (Mark 3:14)

WHY IS THE PRESIDENT OF THE CHURCH CALLED A PROPHET?

Because Joseph Smith is thought of by the Mormons as a Prophet of God, the same as the prophets in the Old and New Testaments. The leaders who followed him, from President Brigham Young to David O. McKay, the President today, are also thought of as prophets.

WHAT ARE THE TEMPLES?

They are sacred buildings in which ceremonies and religious instruction are performed, and in which instruction into the ceremonies of the Church is given. They are not public houses of worship, churches or chapels, which are being built by the hundreds around the world. There are only thirteen Mormon temples in use today:

Salt Lake City, Utah
St. George, Utah
Logan, Utah
Manti, Utah
Hamilton, New Zealand
Berne, Switzerland
London, England
Laie, Hawaii
Cardston, Alberta, Canada
Los Angeles, California
Phoenix, Arizona
Oakland, California
Idaho Falls, Idaho

Plans have been approved for three more temples, in Washington, D.C., Provo, Utah and Ogden, Utah.

St. George Temple

Logan Temple

Alberta Temple

Hawaii Temple

Salt Lake Temple

New Zealand Temple

Arizona Temple

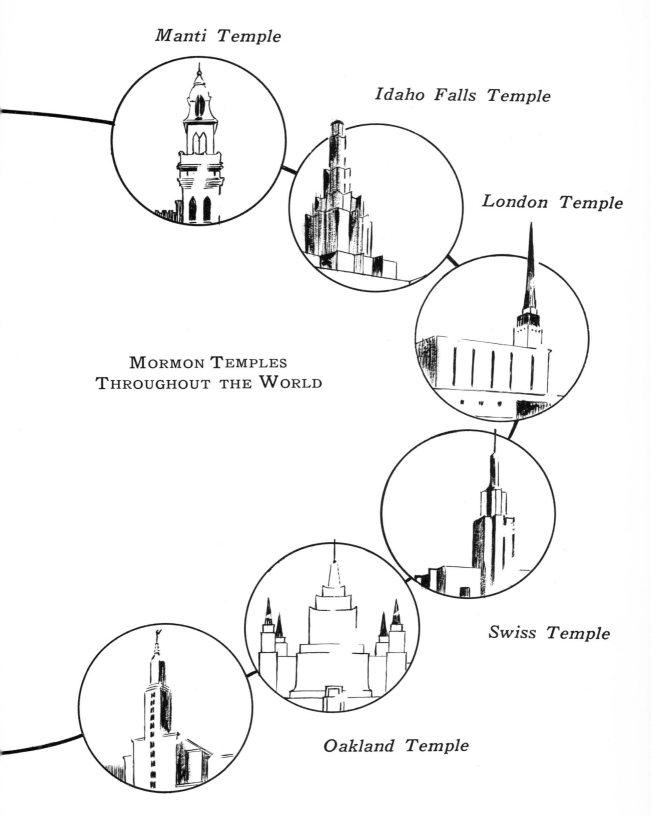

Manti Temple

Idaho Falls Temple

London Temple

MORMON TEMPLES
THROUGHOUT THE WORLD

Swiss Temple

Oakland Temple

Los Angeles Temple

The Mormons

After a temple is dedicated and consecrated, only certain members of the Church are allowed to enter. They must have a written recommendation from their bishop.

Marriages and baptisms are performed in the temples. If a Mormon wishes a deceased member of his family to be baptized into, or married within, the Mormon religion, the living may be baptized or married as representatives of the dead. These ceremonies are performed by "living proxies" for those who died before having a full opportunity to adopt the principles of the gospel. A Mormon believes a just God gives to all who have ever lived an opportunity to hear Him.

Baptismal font in Salt Lake City

Maude Adams'
cradle

What Is the Mormon "Records System"?

Joseph Smith insisted that all such baptisms and marriages performed by living representatives must be done with positive identification of the dead persons.

Thus began a careful record system which today is growing into a fantastic genealogical research library. Information has been, and is being collected from throughout the world . . . birth, marriage, and death certificates.

In the mountains about twelve miles from Salt Lake City is Little Cottonwood Canyon. Its walls are granite; a narrow road leads to one shallow plateau. Here are six concrete entrances; about 150 feet inside, this tunnel is under 800 feet of solid Utah granite. The tunnel leads into a room about 400 feet long and about 50 feet wide. It is lined with corrugated steel, and between it and the granite is waterproofed concrete—the center for the genealogy record!

From the central room three vault doors lead to three 350-foot long rooms. These vaults are self-contained, with all equipment necessary for complete independence. Here, available to the general public, to *anyone* who seeks this information, with complete facilities for their study, are more than 500,000,000 microfilmed records in the Church's genealogical library; these are records of people of all backgrounds, from some twenty countries!

The granite blocks used in the building of the Salt Lake Temple were brought from Little Cottonwood Canyon.

Who Is in the Priesthood?

The President of the Church is the presiding high priest. Within the framework of the priesthood are deacons, teachers, priests, elders, seventies, and high priests.

Every Mormon boy twelve years of age is eligible to hold and serve in some part of the priesthood. There are more than 500,000 in the priesthood.

Are There Mormon Missionaries?

Since the very beginning, in the 1830's, the Church has sent out missionaries to all parts of the world. There were Mormon converts in England before the Saints reached the Salt Lake valley. Today, they are mostly young men of nineteen or twenty, girls over twenty-one, and some older men and women. Mormon missionaries devote two or two-and-a-half years of their lives, at their own or their family's expense, to their task; they give up jobs and school, and leave their families to spread the gospel.

All of the young men who "go out" are ordained into the Melchizedek Priesthood.

Do Mormons Divorce?

They discourage it completely. Only the President of the Church can grant what is called a "Temple divorce."

Do Mormons Baptize?

Yes, by immersion. But the Saints believe in baptism only for those over eight years, when they have become "accountable."

Do Mormons Believe in the Bible?

Yes; the King James version is used officially within the Church.

Does the Church Tithe?

Yes; a tenth of the individual's income—the scriptural tenth:

"Bring ye all the tithes into the storehouse, that there may be meat in mine house, and prove me now herewith, saith the Lord of hosts, if I will not open you the windows of heaven, and pour you out a blessing, that there shall not be room enough to receive it." (Malachi 4:10)

How do Mormons Marry?

A Mormon may be married in a civil ceremony, "until death do us part." A true Mormon marriage is performed in a temple; this is for "time and eternity."

In the temple the bride and groom, dressed in white, kneel at the altar. By the Holy Priesthood, they are married for all eternity. Thus, if they live worthy lives, the family unit will continue into eternity.

What Does the Mormon Church Think About Liquor and Tobacco?

The "Word of Wisdom," a code of health conduct, issued in 1833, was strongly against the use of liquor, tobacco, tea and coffee. The Word says that man should abstain from all injurious things, to further enjoy all of the good things the Lord has provided on earth.

BASIC CHURCH ORGANIZATION

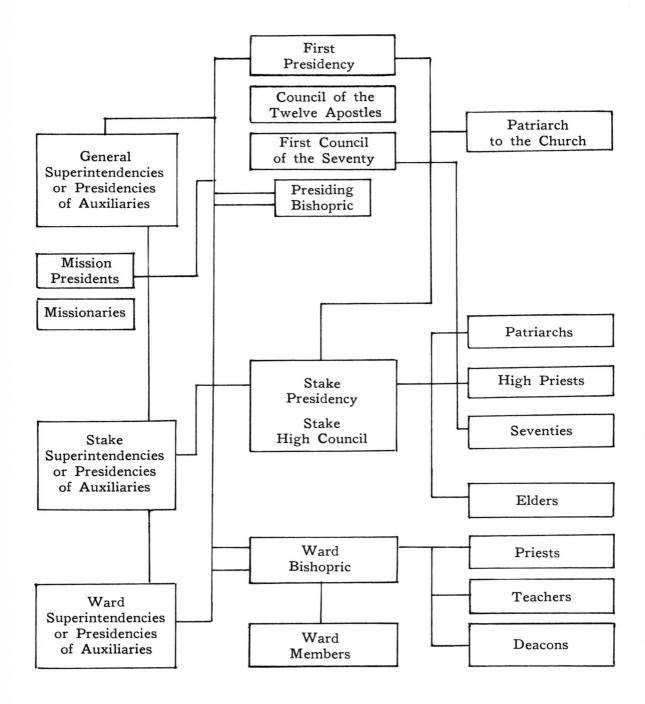

The MORMONS *Today*

The Church today is world-wide. It began with one man; there were forty thousand when the Saints started for Salt Lake valley, and today it is reaching for a membership of three million. There are twelve thousand missionaries in sixty-five countries.

From the beginning, the Church taught the principles of work and self-reliance, as necessary today as it was for the pioneer of the last century. The early Mormon worked to build a temple or a city; the modern Mormon gives time, money, energy and ability for the equivalent ends today. Modern Saints have been encouraged to "put by" food, clothing, and other essentials so that in a difficult time of sickness, unemployment, or hardship, each family can sustain itself.

So, following its principle for the individual, the Church has set up a welfare program to help and provide for any Saints who cannot take care of themselves. For example, various projects are conducted by the Church to raise, produce, and store food, and to manufacture clothing and other items.

The present Mormon Church Welfare Program was set up during the depression, in 1936, by Heber J. Grant, then President of the Saints. Federal relief for Mormons in Utah was not necessary. The program grew from those depression years, through World War II, and today the Church and its local congregations own more than five hundred welfare projects, valued at more than $40,000,000.

All of these items of necessity are stored in what are known as the "bishop's storehouses." * In Salt Lake City one such storehouse sits on a whole block in Welfare Square. It keeps one million cans of vegetables in stock most of the time; meat from the west, and a tremendous cellar for potatoes, carrots, and other root crops.

Towering over Welfare Square is a grain storage elevator which can hold 140 carloads of wheat. It was built in the early months of World War II in just eight days by 640 volunteers who mixed and poured concrete around the clock.

Every Mormon devotes time to these plans, and of course without pay; it is for the good of the total community. The Church has about 650 farms and ranches, 30 canneries, a fleet of trucks, a coal yard, blanket and clothing mills, a soap factory and a coal mine. Volunteer workers gather food and other materials from these Church-wide storehouses for delivery to needy homes.

After World War II, Mormons sent tons of supplies to Europe, and to South America and Greece, following disasters of floods and earthquakes. The Church maintains a hospital system in three western states, the largest of which, in Salt Lake City, has five hundred beds.

Another phase of the Welfare Program is "Deseret Industries," which employs aged or handicapped workers in many workrooms and shops, reclaiming donated toys, clothes, and

---

* A bishop watches over his "ward"; when he sees trouble or need, he has the authority to write out a bishop's order. This permits the bearer to get anything needed, without question, from the "bishop's storehouse." See also Church organization chart.

appliances. These items are sold at minimal prices or donated to those in need.

Two organizations provide cultural and recreational activities for Mormon youth over twelve years of age: the Young Men's and the Young Women's Mutual Improvement Associations, called the M-I-A. These give supervised activities of instruction in drama, speech, music, dance, arts and crafts, sports and athletics.

The Young Men's Association conducts the largest church-sponsored Boy Scout program in the world, in proportion to church membership.

There is also the Relief Society, participated in by more than 260,000 women in the Church. They care for the sick, visiting homes, and helping the families of the sick. They join to can food items to be used for needy families in the welfare program.

Brigham Young University, with more than 23,000 students, is the largest church-operated university in the United States. Utah, about 70% of its population Latter-day Saints, leads all of the states in the union by a large margin in proportion of college students to total population. Also, Utah has produced, in proportion to population, more men in the fields of science and education than any other state. (See list of Some Famous American Mormons.)

All of these activities in the field of education and welfare were begun soon after the pioneers reached the valley in 1847, and have continued and grown, within the framework of their religion, over this brief span of years, to a world-wide, superbly organized Church program.

Eagle Gate,
    at entrance
    to Brigham Young's house

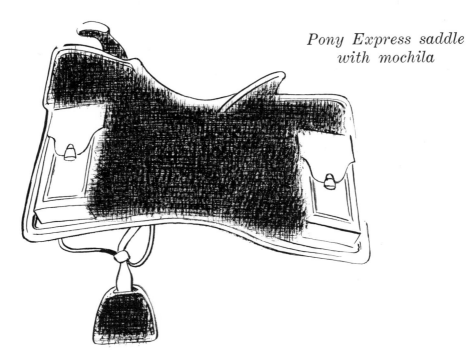

*Pony Express saddle
with mochila*

Of the Nineteenth Century

MAUDE ADAMS (1870–1926) — One of the most famous
of American actresses, Miss Adams made her debut in the
historic Salt Lake Theater at the age of seven weeks. Her
mother, Annie Adams Kiskadden, was a popular leading
lady. One evening, when the baby in her play became ill,
she brought in her own baby daughter. At the age of twenty,
this baby was playing leading roles in theaters all over the
country.

EZRA TAFT BENSON (1811–1869) — It was largely
through his spirit of daring and adventure that the Union
Pacific Railroad came through on time for the union of the
trans-continental line.

90

GEORGE Q. CANNON (1827–1901) — A versatile and talented Utah pioneer, he was a Representative in Congress for Utah Territory, a prolific writer and editor, and a financial advisor and banker for the Church.

J. REUBEN CLARK, JR. (1871–1961) — United States ambassador to Mexico; noted authority on international law; lecturer and author.

WILLIAM CLAYTON (1814–1879) — Poet, historian and musician, he wrote the hymn, "Come, Come Ye Saints"; secretary and confidant to the Prophet Joseph Smith.

KARL G. MAESER (1828–1901) — First president of Brigham Young University (Academy), now the largest church-sponsored university in America.

PARLEY P. PRATT (1807–1857) — Historian; legislator; publisher; scientist. His services as geographer were of great value to the Mormon pioneers on their trek across the trackless plains.

JOSEPH RIDGES (1827–1914) — An English contractor and organ builder who built the world-famous Mormon Tabernacle organ.

ORIN PORTER ROCKWELL (1815–1879) — Once bodyguard for the Prophet Joseph Smith and Brigham Young, this frontiersman performed countless feats of heroism in the early history of the Great Basin territory. His courage as an overland mail and Pony Express rider is legendary.

JOHN A. WIDTSOE (1872–1952) — A noted educator and scientist; president of Utah State College and the University of Utah; internationally acclaimed chemist.

WILFORD WOODRUFF (1807–1898) — Founder of the largest genealogical society in the world (The Genealogical Society, Church of Jesus Christ of Latter-day Saints); fourth president of the Church. His memorable "Manifesto" ended the practice of polygamy among the Mormons.

BRIGHAM YOUNG (1801–1877)—Successor to Joseph Smith as president and prophet of the Mormon Church. A born leader and brilliant colonizer, he led the Mormons across the plains in a remarkable exodus. He laid out and established more than 250 towns and cities in the Great Basin territory.

Of the Present Day

EZRA TAFT BENSON—Attained international renown as an administrator of the food relief program during and following World War II; Secretary of Agriculture in the Eisenhower cabinet.

T. ROY BROADBENT —President of the American Society of Plastic and Reconstruction Surgeons.

JACK DEMPSEY—Former world's heavyweight boxing champion.

HENRY EYRING—Holder of the National Medal of Science; former president of the National Chemistry Society.

HARVEY FLETCHER—Former director of research, Bell Telephone Company; world authority on acoustics and communications; member of the U.S. Academy of Science.

STEPHEN HARVEY FLETCHER—President of Western Electric Company.

ROSEL H. HYDE—Chairman of the Federal Communications Commission.

DAVID M. KENNEDY—Secretary of the Treasury in the Nixon cabinet.

HARMON KILLIBREW—One of the super-stars of baseball.

ROBERT C. KIRKWOOD—President of the F. W. Woolworth Company.

VERNON LAW — Former pitcher and now a coach with the Pittsburgh Pirates; twice was the National League's leading pitcher and winner of two World Series games against the New York Yankees.

DON LIND — One of the first American astronauts.

J. WILLIAM MARRIOT — Founder-president of Hot Shoppes Restaurant chain and national hotel builder and operator.

RAY C. NEEDHAM — USN retired; former commander-in-chief, the U.S. Pacific Fleet.

CHASE PETERSON — Dean of Admissions, Harvard Medical College.

IVY BAKER PRIEST — One of the few women to hold this position, Mrs. Priest was Treasurer of the United States in the Eisenhower Administration.

GEORGE W. ROMNEY — Secretary of Housing and Urban Development in the Nixon cabinet; former governor of Michigan, and president of American Motors.

MORRIS K. UDALL — Esthusiastic and devoted worker for reclamation; U.S. Congressman from Arizona.

STEWART L. UDALL — Brother of Morris; served as Secretary of the Interior of the Kennedy and Johnson cabinets.

OX YOKE

BIBLIOGRAPHY

Charles Coulson Rich, Pioneer Builder of the West by John Henry Evans. The Macmillan Company, New York.

Joseph Smith's Testimony. The Church of Jesus Christ of Latter-day Saints, Salt Lake City, Utah.

Kingdom of the Saints by Ray B. West, Jr. The Viking Press, New York.

Latter-day Saints, The: The Mormons Yesterday and Today by Robert Mullen. Doubleday & Company, Inc., New York.

Life Story of Brigham Young, The by Susan Young Gates. Jarrod's, Publishers, London.

Meet the Mormons by Doyle and Randall Green. Deseret Press, Salt Lake City, Utah.

Mormon Establishment, The by Wallace Turner. Houghton Mifflin Company, Boston, Mass.

Mormons, The: Their Westward Trek by Kate B. Carter. Daughters of Utah Pioneers, Salt Lake City, Utah.

Nauvoo, Kingdom on the Mississippi by Robert Bruce Flanders. University of Illinois Press, Urbana, Illinois.

Pictorial History of Protestantism by Vergilius Ferm. Philosophical Library, New York.

Relic Tells Its Story, A by Kate B. Carter. Daughters of Utah Pioneers, Salt Lake City, Utah.

Story of Telegraphy, The by Kate B. Carter. Daughters of Utah Pioneers, Salt Lake City, Utah.

Utah and the Pony Express by Kate B. Carter. Daughters of Utah Pioneers, Salt Lake City, Utah.

INDEX

Spinning Wheel